A FEW WORDS OF A LOVE BIRD

PYAR KE PANCHHI KE KUCHH SHABD

SHWETA ASHOK VISPUTE

ISBN 979-888521731-6

Contents

Contents

Foreword

Awaiting Hopes for Response from Readers

Hey buddy, Shweta meets. My pleasured heart presents my lively thoughts and sweet dreams before you my dear developed minds of teenagers in the related fields and of likely psychology. Let's go with the flow.

I thought once that if an ant can climb the highest peak then how can't a man fulfill his wishes of growing towards the sky and travelling across the space and flying beyond the limitations of the vast universe; tackling all the ups and downs and kicking every upcoming difficulty of such a long, harsh and versatile life.

I caught it, that's my desire; when I got it what to do in the life forever. Hurdles in my path – my foe, I was never upset with it; friends, the shadow of my work is the signature impression of my personality in which I believe. Sense of poetry is the photocopy of invoking emotions moulded in my heart.

I never believe in stretching the feelings in words. Such is my Mom's young angel, myself; the Mom stitched me in a thread of inspiration and moulded me to give the upcoming outcome of my literature work.

What I put forward is aimed at to do proper justice with the overall roaming and rolling thinking in my mind and I hope I give you what you all deserve, nothing else.

The work of composing poems I have started with the arising tender hopes of growing ambitions of success. At this very moment, sprouting words emerging from the depth of my soul are still 'awaiting hopes'.

Preface

Parents' Words

Her sword of words speaks, we believe. Her creative ideas in each and every poem brought her feelings alive. Each poem is the true resemblance of the floating emotions over the ocean of beats and flourishing in the corner of her heart and the mirror image of her feelings. Every poem is uniquely defined and carry the meaning of its kind. Thoughtful writing with depth and sincere efforts are the proofs of her efficiency to nurture the words to make the poem very effective. Its proud to write something that really means to the poet what it reflects. We appreciate the way she moulded the poems to come out with the best of the creation. Even you can judge a poet as she has opened the heart full of knowledge, so, we can say that what she has given is to be secured to reach her great heights. It is a great pleasure to focus on or spot the continuous devotion of a poet, which we have done from many, hence, we feel good to write here about her work and put forth our personal views.

It is not to end here but the beginning of all the upcoming sessions which will surely be conducted in praise of a newly born poet with her tender and invaluable lines.

Best luck for the future and wholeheartedly supported.

Acknowledgements

I wish to say that ...

I am Shweta Ashok Vispute, BE Computer, KCES's COEM, Jalgaon, undertake that I have composed 37 English poems on various topics. I am very keen to avail me with the opportunity to expose and disclose my poetry and get pleasure after people read my literature. I expect complete support from you if my work deserves. I am strongly willing to continue, with my complete dedication towards my composition, through a chance expected to be given by you.

The literature "A Few Words of a Love Bird" is completely and purely written by me. 100 % of the composition under the title mentioned above is in my own words and by my heart. No word of any of the poem is copied in any way from any other literature or book or taken from any other source. I assure you that all the poems composed by me are the constructive and true impression of my own mind and my own feelings. So, believe it to be reliable.

So, it is hoped that you will further proceed it without any hurdle or obstruction. Trust is must and that I give you. Kindly pay your personal attention to my work. Awaiting for your immediate and favourable consideration to my sincere efforts to secure more creative talents.

Hoping for your kind co-operation. Thanking you.

Yours sincerely,

Shweta Ashok Vispute

Chapter1

Thirst

Nothing is eternal in this world, then what's tempting man ?

What will you carry when you die ? Then, for what will achieve today's running man ?

What are you chasing ? What are you dying for ?

In this 21st century, I don't know; why is the man so much crazy for ?

What is there to follow ? Is there any end to his eternal wants ?

When there is everything he wishes in this decade, then what else he wants ?

He is trying to catch what, when what he demands, he can have

Sky is at his foot if he strongly desires anything to have

Chapter2

The Orphan Opens His Heart

Why not anybody ? Who is there for us ?

Alone but live together with the relation of orphans

No mother. How is father ? Family is unknown.

Nobody to love and care. Our existence is only of our own, alone.

Love, only love we want. Else what are we missing and thirsty for ?

Don't we deserve a smile and parents for whom our eyes are waiting for ?

Somebody love us and walk hand-in-hand, we hope so

Our determination can build castles but never home sweet home to go

Chapter3

Definition of Life

Life is so long whereas life is so short for some

How to define life is a question troublesome

It is a journey from where to start and where to reach, we don't know

To achieve destination is the only aim with which we go and go

The route is so far, to where we are going is not known

Intention is to explore what is yet unknown

With the purpose of studying life, we travel through the way of life

But can only say that the struggle of life is as sharp as knife

What we got and what we not about life is still not sure

Even after taking all the knowledge about it, life is such that we can't explore

Power of life can't be understood

We have to follow its path whether we not or in mood

To end with, life is mischievous

Helplessly, we have to accept with patience what it gives to us

Chapter4

Belief in Possibility

People cry, I don't know why

When everything is possible then instead, why don't try

A thought that its impossible if possess the mind

Its a very dangerous misunderstanding of its kind

Nothing is impossible, believe in it

A 'Will' will find a way, its a belief tight

"I'm possible" is hidden in impossible

If you persue then any critical situation, you can handle

Thorough thinking tells me that

Positive thoughts never deceive infact

What I want to say, here I complete

Belief in possibility is must, hope you get it

Chapter5

The Truth
Bitter the truth, but not so
Say it or not, don't get confused bro
To speak it, smilingly go ahead
Don't hesitate, believe in what you said
May people angry or poke fun of it
Never alter your way, don't divert from what good you did
Be honest, be truthful; happen whatever will
Open your heart, give all your sincerity with your own will
Be true-hearted, diminish all the troubles
Truth leads, lie never overcomes

Chapter6

What I Feel

What I feel, never unmasked

Kept hidden, in the corner of a heart

Whole life played hide and seek

Not to reveal what I feel deep

Will protect the secret rest of life

Nurture secretly in the heart to take a sigh of relief

What I feel, I never say; yet not exposed

Frighten to disclose, whatever in my mind goes

One day, at one time; O Simon

What I feel, God knows, will wide open ?

Chapter7

What I Feel in Dream
What a face, what a smile
Let me look, for a while
That's you, what a view
What an effect, on my heart; it will give
Lovely eyes, eye-catching sight
Heart-charming lips; in them, heart-touching delight
O beauty, what's your name
To love you, that's my forever aim
If I am not mistaken, that's love
Hence, what I feel; is so natural
When I was awaken, I found it
A sweet dream, on a bed indeed

Chapter8

A Vivid Memory
I remember well that vivid memory
Unforgettable incident of life's journey
She told me, she is expecting
Soon we will have a lovely kid in the home playing
Unaware was I, brought by destiny here
That horrible day, I will forget never
Doctor told me about the complications
She will die if she gives birth to a child after operation
Uncertainty loomed me, I thought so
What the Almighty wants, who knows
Again, in a while; I caught the only feeling
If I go in a temple and vow, then ok will be everything
I rushed to it to do so
Hope I will find some temple near to go
Until I finish my visit, a news broke into my ears
A positivity is shown in delivery by your wife dear
A very cute life took new birth
When I took in hands, little eyes stunning at the father's shirt
My cheer knew no bounds at his glance
What a memorial day; to live for him, my supposed to death life
just a time before, got a new chance

Chapter9

Friendship

Two are attached, affection is there

One is happy, if other is fair

It's a promise, not a relation mere

Friendship is a lovely bond, established between more or pair

Love is there for each, with everybody's equal share

To give one's life for one, one can dare

Sacrifice is here, which is more than care

Breakup is only for the period of nightmare

Chapter10

Marriage

Tie a bond sacred, uprising age
Knot the two to overcome loneliness
Event is so useful, part of life
Get arranged with a beautiful wife
Give her love, she only demands
Forever and ever for which she asks
Trust is must, remember well
Union of two hearts is necessary for survival

Chapter11

What to do ?

No one knows what to do

In ups and downs, tackle how

Here and there, run everywhere

People get confused too

Critics to criticize but have to

Overpower the situation somehow

Beyond the limits of nature

God is there to help you

Chapter12

Philosophy of Love

It is tough to live without love

Love is life and to live for one's life its it's purpose

Love demands nothing except love

Only love it wants each other to serve

There is no place for harsh treatments

It is a lovely smoother bond of sentiments

Truth and sanctity are the principles of love

And faith lies in the lovers' nerves

Chapter 13

Girlfriend got Married

I am sole, I am alone

My heart is deserted, I lost life's tone

Why did you go ? But you had to

I was there waiting but not considered by you

Sun rises daily, night falls on its time

But I find not what is, your beautiful lips with a lovely smile

My hands are anxious to feel your touch

But even to see you smile, I have to ask someone; isn't it too much

Chapter14

What a Youth Feels

I fell in love but yet not matured

I don't know, how such feelings my heart captured

I experience what, I cannot say

Something little different by the way

I am scared, what has happened

Now I always feel anxious to see your eyes brightened

Whether something has went wrong with me

Obviously, who has escaped from such an age; transformation into young from tiny

Chapter15

Value of Time

Keep in mind
To follow punctually the going time
If you know the importance
You will win the world at once
Timely doing habits help a lot
What I mean have you got ?
Time is precious, more than glory
If you miss it, there is no time to sorry

Chapter16

The Precious Time
Time of life, not to waste
Life is always a walk in haste
Who caught the time is the lucky one
That one is the tomorrow's rising sun
It is difficult to pass the course of time
If you sit idle having wine
Hence, you keep working essentially
Think of its care to use it more importantly

Chapter17

Me - The Farmer

Struggle is my life, all the days pass in toil

Sweating in the schorching heat, I keep working on this soil

Black Earth down and blue sky above

They witness my efforts, I fight with the nature how

My patience tests God to stand the crops

I wait for the rain. When will it come again ? Precious every drop

Its my own motherland, still, I owe debt to money-lender

Every year I smile when grow even a little crop tender

Chapter18

The Sky

High above upwards, from where to where it stretches

Limit and range of its width, no eye catches

Clouds', lightening's shelter

Sequence of sun and rain, no one can alter

Birds and planes are attracted towards its open door

It exists between outer space and Earth; home for sun and moon, stars and many more

Events of day and night take place

In the darkness where the sun hides, we cannot chase

Such a sky is the only one

No new wonder, it fascinates and is awesome

Chapter19

What a Disciple says

What I am, because of you

A learner learnt every word from thou

I didn't know the difference between sun and moon

You told me how to react to the situations as soon

My ignorance vanished, my mind enlightened with knowledge

A to Astronomy, I got it from you, I acknowledge

Beloved disciple always follow your sincere path

Thanks to you, I owe debt of my life, my soul; teacher-student relationship is a form of God's art

Chapter20

Psychology - A Question

To describe the philosophy of psychology, many thoughts come in my mind

What to consider and what to say, I don't understand and determine

It's a topic vast, concept elaborate

How to trace the mind and follow the meaning of sequence of words, I can't concentrate

It confuses me, I cannot solve the puzzle of psychology

Who will read whose's mind, yet has made no such technology

It puts a question mark on my brain

All efforts to catch its logic of mine are gone in vain

Chapter21

The Great Shivaji

My ideal icon is Shivaji Maharaj

With great efforts who fought for 'Hindavi Swaraj'

He was the one who cut the tail of Mughals

He took oath to vanish the Mughal empire's survival

He diminished their strength and brought them to end

Anyhow, he wanted to fulfill the dream of his mother to live independent

He lived for the country, struggled for the motherland

He followed the path of mythological heroes; my dear children, such was his life. Do you understand ?

Chapter22

The Nature

Friend and foe is nature

Many things it gives helpful and why it snatches more through

natural calamities, I don't understand being mature

Man depends on it for whole life for all things

To each man, it treats equally whether be queen or king

If it comes to its anger, then all get afraid

Beware of its harsh nature, someone has said

It takes none of a second, to destroy you

If you keep yourself in limit, that's better for you

It's a God's gift, preserve it well

Die for it, take care and same to others tell

Chapter23

To whom I Respect

Greater than God, they give heavenly pleasure

To a child, their warmth goes to infinity, we can't measure

Love is limitless, demands nothing

A child's smile is enough and everything

Such an affection even God needs

But its only for their beloved child

Range of love is beyond horizon of heart

What a style of love, only for their body's part

Chapter24

Patient's Life
Poor their life, on a bed
No colour seems, only blood red
Nurses to serve and doctor to cure
Still their life remain or depart, its not sure
People to help and care but precaution is must
None other than doctor, a patient trusts
He saves lives and relieves pain
He gives a sigh of relief to a patient's vein
He is a source of hope, inspires life to live; moreover, his efforts are there for patient's every breath
But sorry to say, he can't overcome the cruel death

Chapter25

Loving Success, Teasing Defeat

Successful life, successful heart give you the charm and a smile on your face

Struggle is life and defeat is stepping stone of success in life's race

If you win, you get showers of flowers

Just a single failure, depress millions of your well-wishers

Life is sometimes two sides of coin

Sequence of winning and losing go in processing

All to say is that all is well

Just you succeed in life, never fail

Chapter26

Divine Belief

Faith in God is the utmost need of life

Believe in or not; without his blessings, you cannot survive

He is almighty, he is devotional power

From birth to death, he rules our life with care; such love on man, no other than the creator showers

He excuses us, he forgives us if we are at innocent fault

He is kind to man; our wrong deed mistakenly done, if we confess he considers not

He is everywhere but keep him in soul

He lives in the man's heart because to his interest, he finds no place on the Earth whole

Chapter27

Loss of Manly Feelings

To pay sympathy is human

Then why humanity is lost, a curse became a person

To spread good thoughts, such a longing no longer remained

Man turned inhuman, he proved himself an animal, his image no longer maintained

He forgot the meaning of his life

Why was he made ? To serve other's life

His heart is for love and his soul is for devotion

Man should live for man, brotherhood is his life's only purpose or of his creation

Chapter28

Comparison between Two

Independence of a bird to fly high astonishes my looks

Why doesn't it remain on Earth ? We neither tie its freedom nor it

has any binding to reach the sky, this thought I undertook

To search for food or to make a haste for a drop of water

Sometimes, I feel and don't hesitate to say that my life is better

To think of its lifespan afraids me

Man live long but helpful for no while, see

A little life to a little bird

Whereas in its life, I hope not but sure; many lives a bird has cheered

Comparison of the two gives what

Who is closer to God, happier and satisfied; I cannot conclude that

Chapter29

Once upon a Time

Once upon a time, I saw a little angel

It looked pretty, cool from foot to head overall

Her dress was like a fairy sweet

And her face was like a baby doll

Where was it until now ?

I don't know her name at all

When I hugged, then she laughed

It was none other than my baby small

Chapter30

My Loving Child

You are my sigh, you are my breath; your sensation in my feelings lies

My loving child, I always want you in front of my eyes

You go far, I feel insecure

You live in my heart; my love, my relief, my child you are

I care for you, I worry for you; I don't imagine you get hurt

Afterall, bearing all the pain; I gave you birth

Keeping all the world aside, I think of you

Infront of me always are your eyes blue

You are my shadow, dearest of all my sweetheart

I see your face in every flower, you are traced in my heart

Chapter 31

Sun verses Wind

I am powerful, more than you

You blow and blow, I shine in the sky above

I give people brightness, prove yourself greater, I ask you, I challenge you

Trees inhale, people breathe, I am better, what is there just to remain in the sky above

To answer you, even I reach the heights of Earth and fly in the sky

Don't dare to compare me, my limitations are not only vast but also no one knows from someone's hand I escape why

Your schorching heat teases people, I give them cool breeze

My velocity of flowing, no one can cease

To my side is much more, I am infinite if you measure and impossible to capture

You are constant at one place, just a circle high upwards, none other than a hot creature

Listen bro, don't boast

We both are important most

Perhaps, if I don't shine for a day

How will the world survive in the darkness, say ?

Plants synthesize their food, on plants, web of life depends

Message of my importance, through its ways, timely, the nature sends

Universe needs me, think over it

There is a reason for which the Almighty has created my might

Chapter 32

Love for Birthday Boy

A ray of emotion evoked from my heart with lots of hopes bright

A fountain of feelings scattered to pray for your long life, full of light

Focus of happiness and joy concentrate on you not only for today

May come ever and ever this very special day

Filled with colours and many smiles on your face always

We wish you celebrate all enlightened birthdays

All the angels and heaven wish my angel Shubham

To cheer your birth anniversary, this universe breaks the mum

Chapter33

My Wishes

May God shower his blessings on you

Live long life dear Mom's princess, with all I wish too

Flowers are praying for you today

May the nature always care for you, stars say

Hope this fine day give you a lot from life

My love, you are an only cutie pie blessed of its type

Friends and dear ones love you a lot

May this special day come everyday, they always thought

Such a precious moment is only for you

Hope I get a chance lakhs of times to wish you

I miss this sweet day whole year

From a deep heart, again a very happy birthday to you my dear

Hope this day come again and again

Even, you feel so special ever; such a longing, I don't know I feel since when

Chapter34

Natural Shower

Shower from sky, what we call it as rain

All my thoughts to catch it in hands go in vain

What to say, from infant to aged love it

Such a natural water, even the nature feel in heart for it

Who is the architect of nature, I thought one day

From many of its surprises, rain is one of the best of its way

I don't know, in it what's so strange

That people go crazy even a drop falls and rainbow occurs in the sky's range

It's glittering water catches my eyesight

Secret behind the beauty of this natural shower, I can't describe it

Chapter35

Art of Living

Let's go with the flow but this is not art of living

To love adventures and dare to overcome the problems of life is the most important thing

Creator created us not to cry

Then, some people quit to live the life why

Don't leave to live even someone passes

If someone is born, then how the death anyone can escape

We learn this, just a smile win lots of hearts

Who learnt the secrets of life and tried to aware of its nature is a guy smart

To inhale is an art of life but to live happily is an art of living

What else a man wants except it, it is what today's every person missing

Chapter36

Money is Honey

What's so tempting the world ? Obviously, none other than money

Man is dying for it. Is there other influencing truth of this century any ?

Love lost its importance because of it

It's the only reason that man forgot his blood relations complete

Now, money is honey; my heart says

My beats stop if I don't get a glimpse of it everyday

Such a poor situation of today's become

Its craze, now a days, no one can overcome

It fascinates, so, made man mad

Because of it, the condition of today's man has become so sad

Chapter37

The Terror

No one can understand the depth of a child's innocence

Then, why such innocence turns into terrorism ? Is there really any sense ?

Are choosing or forced to choose the path

What's the truth ? What's the reality ? But terrorists should be kept from the society apart.

They deserve sympathy or to be hanged till death

Kill many innocents, I feel why do they exist yet ?

'Terrorism – The Terror' is a pollution of cruels, they are not humans

They cross every level of cruelty. If they are allowed to live, then there is no solution to terrorism

They are stone-hearted, bad-minded even wicked soul which are live examples of devils

In the heart having no goodwill, such stubborn evils

I think, there is no comment on the topic forward if thought of forgiveness capture the mind

Because I am helpless to say that to these inhumans, no relation can truly bind

How it should be brought to end and uprooted completely from the society, it puts a question mark

As in the form of man, I experience that their teeth of sin are dangerous than that of wild sharks

They give intolerable torture and long lasting ill-effects when attack, to remember forever

Why shy ? What shame ? No mercy from them. They are guilty after commiting any sin never

No God. No Lord. Only born and believe to kill

My belief is that none other than the terrorism I hate so much and frighten to deal

www.ingramcontent.com/pod-product-compliance
Lightning Source LLC
Chambersburg PA
CBHW041652150726

48005CB00013BA/1701